A Child's First Library of Learning

Our Bodies

TIME-LIFE BOOKS • ALEXANDRIA, VIRGINIA

Contents

Why Aren't Girls' Bodies The Same as Boys'?

ANSWER When boys grow up they become men. Men and boys are males. When girls grow up they become women. Women and girls are females. Males and females come together and mate to produce babies. Since males and females play different roles in reproduction, their bodies are designed differently. That is why girls' and boys' bodies are different.

■ Male and female animals

▲ **Lions.** A lion and a lioness. The lion has a mane.

▲ **Beetles.** This male has a horn on its head.

Changes in men and women

Men have deeper voices.

Men can grow beards on their faces.

And their bodies are wider and taller.

A woman's voice doesn't change when she grows up.

Women have less body hair and don't grow beards.

Their bodies are more curvy and they have breasts.

● To the Parent

Visible differences between the male and female occur in nearly all species of the animal kingdom. Though often they are not obvious in the young, the external differences become more noticeable with age. Differences in the reproductive organs of the male and the female are known as primary sexual characteristics. External differences such as the lion's mane and the rooster's comb are secondary sexual characteristics.

Why Do Babies Cry All the Time?

ANSWER When they are small, babies cannot ask for what they want. That's why they cry. They are telling their parents they want something.

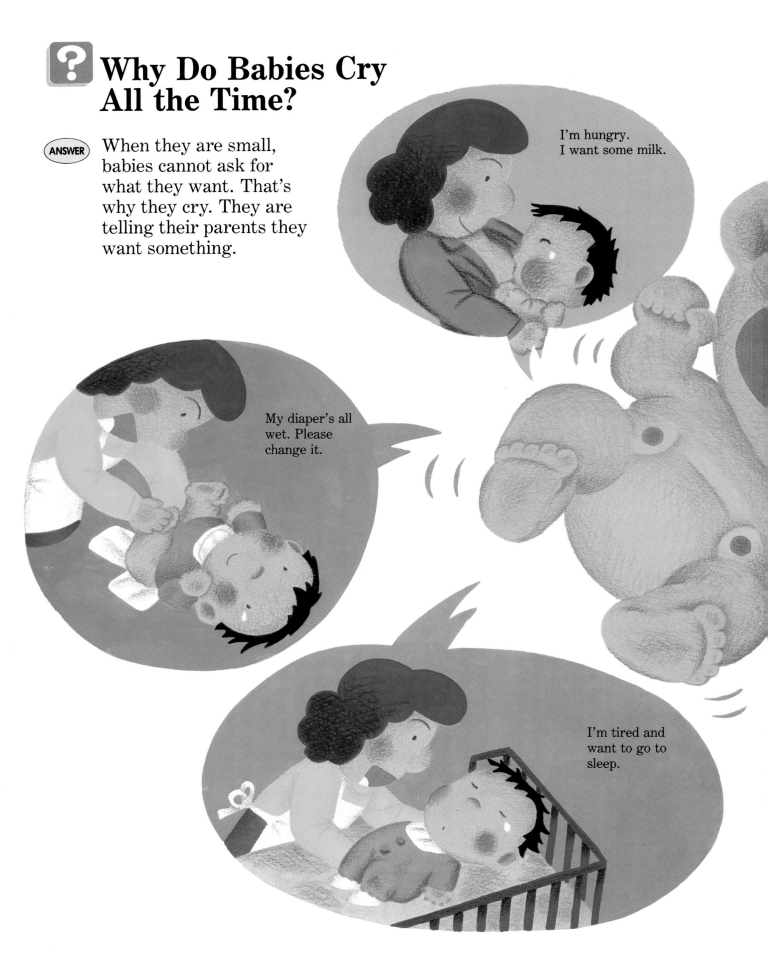

I'm hungry.
I want some milk.

My diaper's all wet. Please change it.

I'm tired and want to go to sleep.

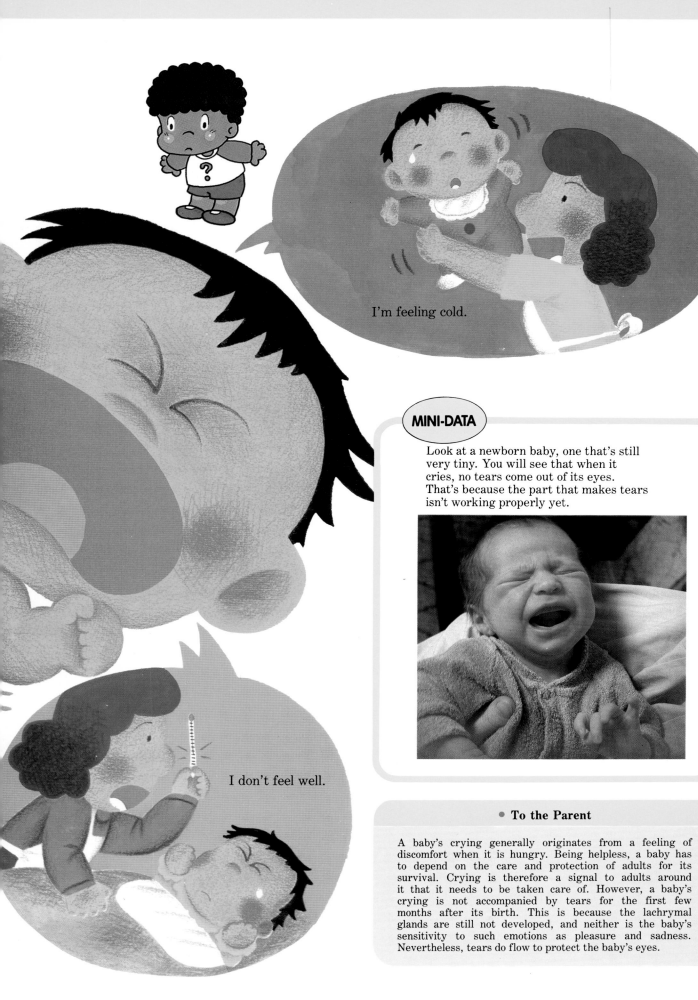

I'm feeling cold.

I don't feel well.

MINI-DATA

Look at a newborn baby, one that's still very tiny. You will see that when it cries, no tears come out of its eyes. That's because the part that makes tears isn't working properly yet.

● To the Parent

A baby's crying generally originates from a feeling of discomfort when it is hungry. Being helpless, a baby has to depend on the care and protection of adults for its survival. Crying is therefore a signal to adults around it that it needs to be taken care of. However, a baby's crying is not accompanied by tears for the first few months after its birth. This is because the lachrymal glands are still not developed, and neither is the baby's sensitivity to such emotions as pleasure and sadness. Nevertheless, tears do flow to protect the baby's eyes.

What Is a Bellybutton?

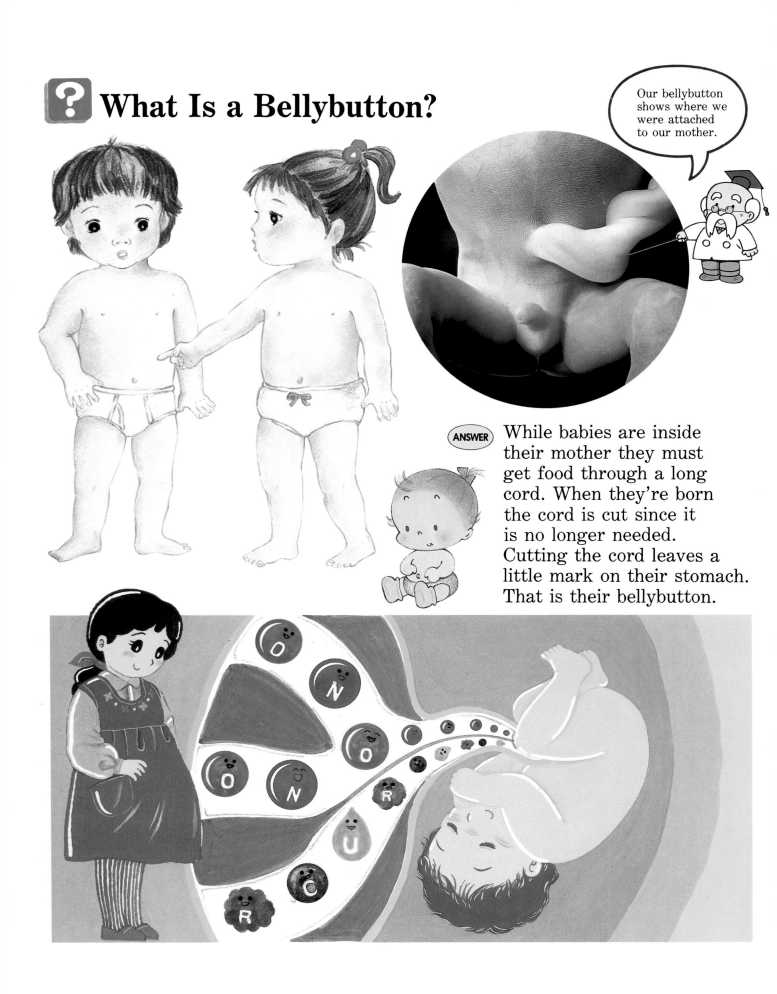

Our bellybutton shows where we were attached to our mother.

ANSWER While babies are inside their mother they must get food through a long cord. When they're born the cord is cut since it is no longer needed. Cutting the cord leaves a little mark on their stomach. That is their bellybutton.

8

Why Do We Get Fluff in Our Bellybutton?

The fluff in your bellybutton is just dirt that collects there. It is hard to get dirt out once it gets in, so you must clean yourself well.

■ Be very gentle with your bellybutton

Your bellybutton is covered with less skin than the rest of your stomach, so if you treat it too roughly it will get sore. When cleaning your bellybutton, be gentle and use a clean cotton swab.

CHECK IT OUT

Dogs and cats grow inside their mothers before they are born, so they have a bellybutton, too. But animals like frogs, which come out of eggs, don't have bellybuttons. Look closely at the animals around you, and find which have bellybuttons and which do not.

● **To the Parent**

When a baby is born, its umbilical cord is clamped off and cut. The stump that is left attached to the infant withers and drops off, leaving the scar known as the navel. The umbilical cord is the baby's lifeline when it is in the womb. It connects the baby to the placenta of the mother and carries nourishment and oxygen from the placenta to the fetus and returns waste from the fetus to the placenta. Just after birth, the cord is removed because it is no longer needed.

Why Does Our Head Have So Much Hair?

ANSWER Inside our head is our brain. It is very important. It keeps our body running perfectly, and it is what we use to think with. All that hair protects our head and brain from bumps, from the sun and from all sorts of other dangers in the world around us.

■ What hair does

If something hits us on the head our hair makes it hurt less.

Just like a pillow!

It stops the sun from making our head too hot when it is very sunny.

Just like an umbrella!

It protects our head if we visit very cold places.

Just like a hat!

10

■ All about hair

Our hair keeps growing, falling out and growing again all the time. The life of a strand of hair is about four or five years for a man and about five or six years for a woman. Our hair falls out and grows again a little at a time. It doesn't all fall out at the same time, and that's why we always have hair on our head.

A man's short hair and a woman's long hair. The life span is almost the same.

■ How fast does hair grow?

Our hair is formed at the hair roots and it is always growing. It is believed that hair grows a half inch (12 mm) each month.

● **To the Parent**

Despite appearances, the body is almost totally covered with hair. We have thicker hair on our head, under our arms and in the pubic area. The rest of the body, except for the palms of our hands, soles of our feet and our lips, is covered by fine, downy hair. The hair on the head is thickest and also grows fastest. There are from 80,000 to 100,000 hairs on the human head. For some reason, women's hair grows faster than men's.

11

❓ Why Does Our Hair Turn Gray?

ANSWER Our hair contains lots of little grains of something called melanin. This is made by the hair roots. As we age they make less of it, and finally none, and that is when our hair turns white.

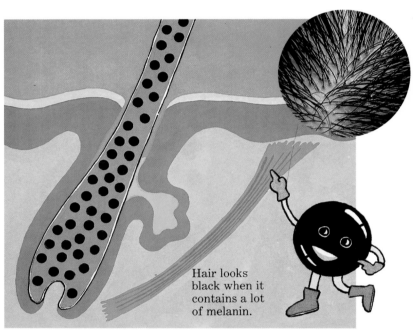

Hair looks black when it contains a lot of melanin.

When hair doesn't contain any melanin, it turns white.

MINI-DATA

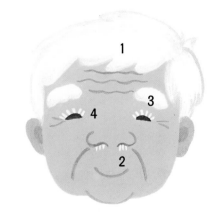

When our hair starts to turn white, the hair of our head turns white first. After that, the hair in our nose turns white, followed by our eyebrows and finally our eyelashes.

Why Do Old Men Lose Their Hair?

When we are young, as soon as our hair falls out, new hair grows back again to take its place. It grows from the roots of the hair. As we get older, the roots of our hair get weaker. They gradually lose the strength to make any new hair.

■ Some men don't go bald

Some men don't go bald even when they grow older. Other men become bald while they are still young. Baldness runs in families.

■ Women don't go bald

Women generally do not lose their hair and go bald even when they get older. That is because the hormones in women's bodies are a little different from those in men's bodies, so women don't become bald the way men do.

Grandfather

Grandfather

Father

Father

• To the Parent

The reason why white hair is shiny is that air has penetrated into the medulla, or inner substance, of the hair and is reflecting light. Graying hair is often hereditary, and this is particularly true of persons whose hair starts turning gray at a very early age.

❓ Why Do We Get a Lump When We Bump Our Head?

ANSWER Just under the skin on our head are lots of little tubes that carry our blood. They are blood vessels. If we bump our head on something, some of these vessels break and the blood flows out. It can't escape, so it makes a bump.

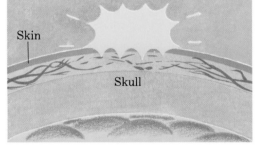

Skin

Skull

▲ When we bump our head hard...

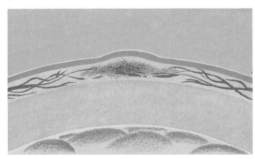

▲ ... the blood starts to come out.

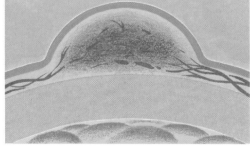

▲ Blood under the skin forms a lump.

14

How Do We Get Bruises?

We get bruises when we bump something with the soft parts of our body. Blood vessels break and blood spills out into the flesh around the bump. It spreads to the skin and shows through, and that is a bruise.

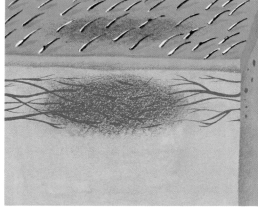

▲ Blood spilling out from broken blood vessels spreads out to form a bruise.

MINI-DATA

Caring for a bruise

If you bump yourself and a bruise starts to form, hurry and put a cold, wet towel on it. That may make it feel better. But keep your fingers away from it. Touching it will not help it. And don't put anything hot on it.

Don't touch it.

No hot towels.

● **To the Parent**

Blood vessels are spread through every part of the body like a fine net. Internal hemorrhaging brought on by contusions will appear as spots of discoloration, sometimes blue and sometimes purple, depending on whether the hemorrhaging is fairly close to the surface of the skin or at a deeper level. Intense bleeding just below the skin causes a swelling called a blood blister.

? Did You Know That Our Eyes Always Have Tears in Them?

ANSWER We always have tears in our eyes. There are some tears there all the time to keep our eyes from getting dry and to help keep them clean.

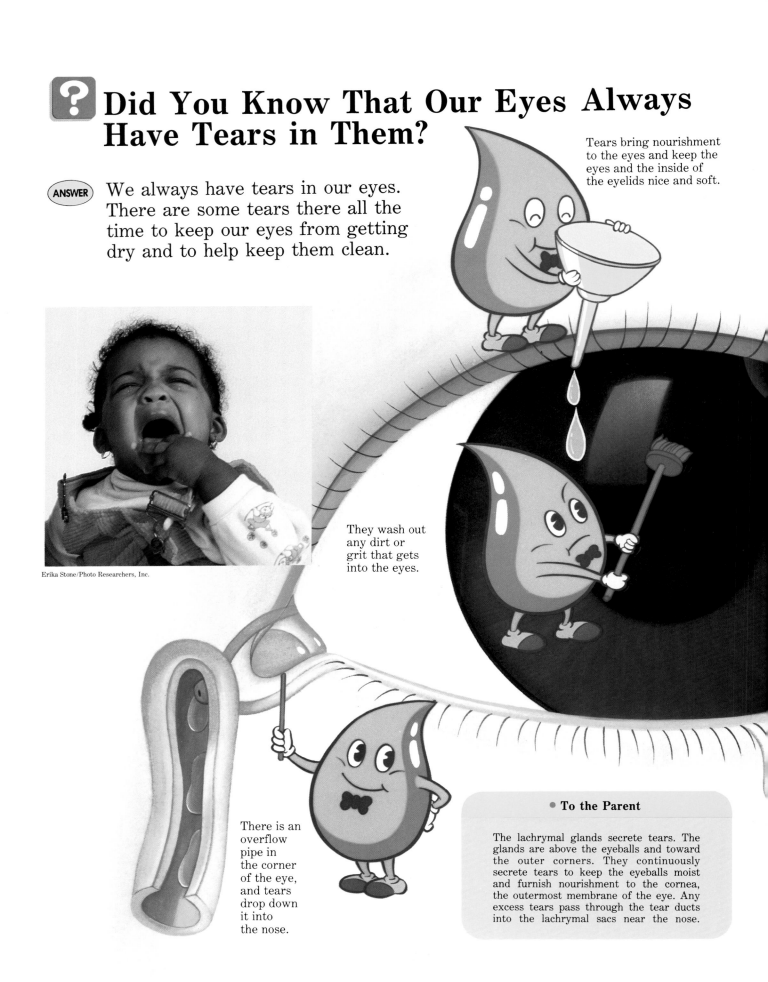

Tears bring nourishment to the eyes and keep the eyes and the inside of the eyelids nice and soft.

Erika Stone/Photo Researchers, Inc.

They wash out any dirt or grit that gets into the eyes.

There is an overflow pipe in the corner of the eye, and tears drop down it into the nose.

● **To the Parent**

The lachrymal glands secrete tears. The glands are above the eyeballs and toward the outer corners. They continuously secrete tears to keep the eyeballs moist and furnish nourishment to the cornea, the outermost membrane of the eye. Any excess tears pass through the tear ducts into the lachrymal sacs near the nose.

We have glands in our upper eyelid

This is where tears are produced.

Tears protect the eyes from germs.

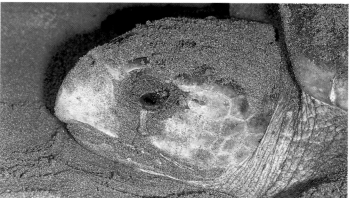

▲ **Sea turtles.** The big reptiles look as if they are crying, but really it is only that they have too much salt in their eyes, and they are getting rid of it.

▲ **Snakes.** These creatures have eyes that are covered by a thin membrane, which is rolled back in this picture. Snakes do not shed tears as people do.

MINI-DATA

We blink very often but may not realize it. We blink to wash our eyes with tears. Blinking also keeps our eyeballs from getting too dry.

We also blink when something seems to be about to fly into our eyes. The blink protects the eyes.

How Do Glasses Help Us See?

(ANSWER) As light enters our eye it passes through a lens. When this lens focuses light in just the right spot we can see clearly. But sometimes our lens is the wrong shape or our eye muscles are too weak. Glasses help our lens focus light so that we see clearly.

Without glasses

This is how a garden with flowers and trees may look to someone who needs glasses.

With glasses

When correction is made with glasses, the scene looks much clearer than it did.

■ Here is how our eye works

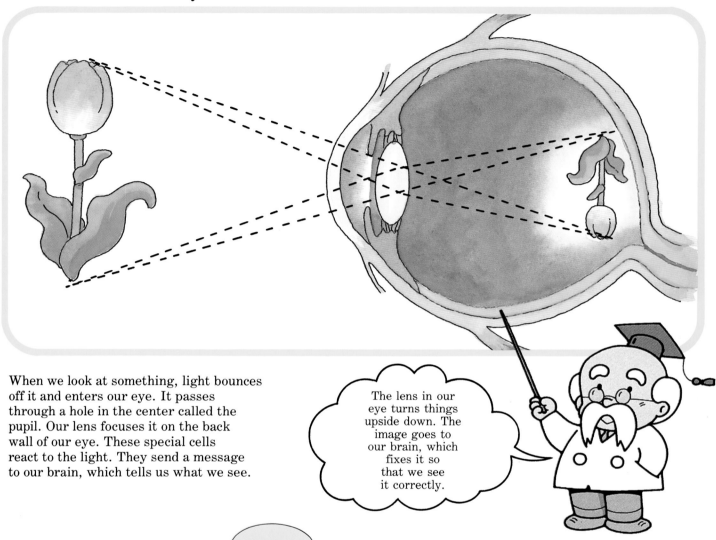

When we look at something, light bounces off it and enters our eye. It passes through a hole in the center called the pupil. Our lens focuses it on the back wall of our eye. These special cells react to the light. They send a message to our brain, which tells us what we see.

The lens in our eye turns things upside down. The image goes to our brain, which fixes it so that we see it correctly.

TRY THIS

Stand near a mirror in a dark room. Then turn on the light. Your pupil will get smaller. That prevents too much light from going into your eye.

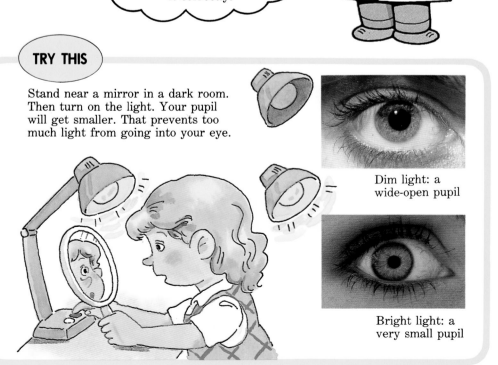

Dim light: a wide-open pupil

Bright light: a very small pupil

? Why Are Our Eyes Set Apart?

ANSWER 1 So we will know the exact position of the things we are looking at. Draw a small circle on a piece of paper. Then close one eye and try to put a dot in the center of the circle. It isn't easy, is it? Now try it with two eyes. Not so hard, is it?

It's really difficult to do it with one eye closed, isn't it?

But it's very easy to do with both eyes open.

ANSWER ❷ It widens our field of vision.

Put your palms together in front of your face. Now with both eyes open and looking straight ahead, move your hands apart. See how far apart you can move them and still be able to see them with both eyes.

Now try doing it with one eye closed. It can be either eye. But notice how the hand that is on the side of the closed eye disappears much faster than it did when you were watching it with two eyes.

TRY THIS

Do it two ways

We use our eyes to help us keep our balance. Try standing on one leg like the boy in this picture. If you do it with both eyes open you can balance on one leg like this for a long time. But if you close one eye, it's really hard to keep your balance, isn't it?

● **To the Parent**

Seeing things in proper perspective and three dimensions is possible only when we can look at them with both eyes. Since our eyes are set apart, we get a slightly different picture out of each. But when the pictures pass through our optical nerves and are merged, we get a three-dimensional view. The area we can see top to bottom and side to side is called our field of vision. Most people have a field of vision about like that in the diagram below.

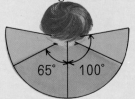

65° 100°

Eyes farther apart make a wider field of vision.

Why Do We Have Two Ears?

ANSWER So that we can guess which direction sound is coming from. We are able to do this without moving our head because we have an ear on each side.

Ears Shaped Like This Pick Up Sounds Best

Ears are shaped just like seashells because that's the best shape for picking up sounds. Put your hand behind your ear like the child in the picture on the right. Now turn your head in the direction of a sound. You can hear much clearer with your hand behind your ear like this, can't you?

MINI-DATA

Cats' ears move all around

Cats can move their ears and turn them in any direction. They can move each ear by itself. This helps them to hear very well.

▲ **Listening to a sound from in front of it**

▲ **Listening to a sound from behind it**

● **To the Parent**

We have an outer ear, an inner ear and a middle ear. What we call our ear is actually the auricle and is part of the outer ear. It catches sounds and passes them to the middle ear, where the eardrum vibrates and relays them to the inner ear. They then pass via the diencephalon, or inner brain, to the auditory center in the cerebral cortex, where they are broken down so that they have particular meanings for us.

Why Do We Get Carsick or Seasick?

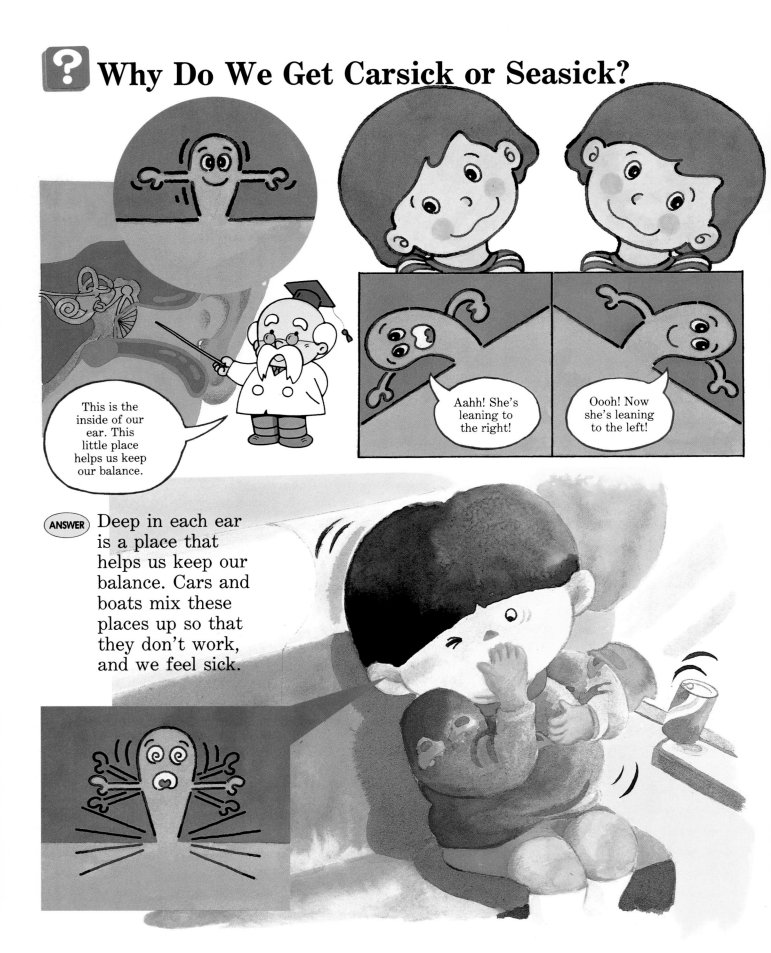

This is the inside of our ear. This little place helps us keep our balance.

Aahh! She's leaning to the right!

Oooh! Now she's leaning to the left!

ANSWER Deep in each ear is a place that helps us keep our balance. Cars and boats mix these places up so that they don't work, and we feel sick.

■ We often get sick in boats or autos

Boats and autos often bounce up and down or go from one side to the other. Those motions upset our balancing system, and then we get sick.

■ So you won't get sick...

Don't eat just before setting out on a trip.

Sleep well the night before a trip.

If you go on a boat trip it will help you keep from getting sick if you look at something far away and not at the surface of the water.

• To the Parent

Two organs in the inner ear keep us balanced. The semicircular canal, three tubes that connect to the vestibule, is sensitive to changes in movement and direction. Changes in the tilt of the angle of the body are sensed by the vestibule. Irregular motions can disturb the normal functions of these organs and might result in one of the various forms of motion sickness.

❓ How Do Our Ears Work?

ANSWER Our ears have three main parts that work together. First, the outer ear captures sounds from the air. Next, the middle ear makes the sounds louder. Finally, the inner ear sends a message to the brain.

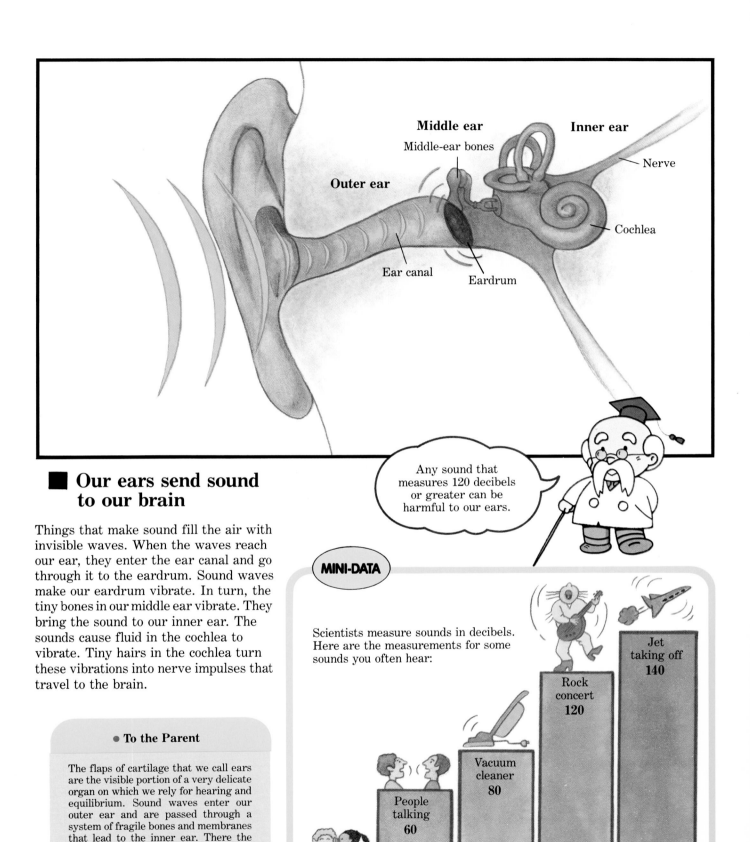

Middle ear
Middle-ear bones

Outer ear

Inner ear

Nerve

Cochlea

Ear canal

Eardrum

■ Our ears send sound to our brain

Things that make sound fill the air with invisible waves. When the waves reach our ear, they enter the ear canal and go through it to the eardrum. Sound waves make our eardrum vibrate. In turn, the tiny bones in our middle ear vibrate. They bring the sound to our inner ear. The sounds cause fluid in the cochlea to vibrate. Tiny hairs in the cochlea turn these vibrations into nerve impulses that travel to the brain.

Any sound that measures 120 decibels or greater can be harmful to our ears.

MINI-DATA

Scientists measure sounds in decibels. Here are the measurements for some sounds you often hear:

Jet taking off **140**

Rock concert **120**

Vacuum cleaner **80**

People talking **60**

Whisper **20**

Decibels

● **To the Parent**

The flaps of cartilage that we call ears are the visible portion of a very delicate organ on which we rely for hearing and equilibrium. Sound waves enter our outer ear and are passed through a system of fragile bones and membranes that lead to the inner ear. There the vibrations are converted to nerve impulses and relayed to the brain for interpretation. The human ear can hear a range of sounds, which scientists measure in decibels.

Why Do Our Ears Pop When We Go Into a Tunnel?

ANSWER Inside our ear is a little tight piece of skin called the eardrum. Usually the air inside the ear presses as hard against the eardrum as the air outside. But in a tunnel the air inside the ear presses harder, and that makes the ear pop.

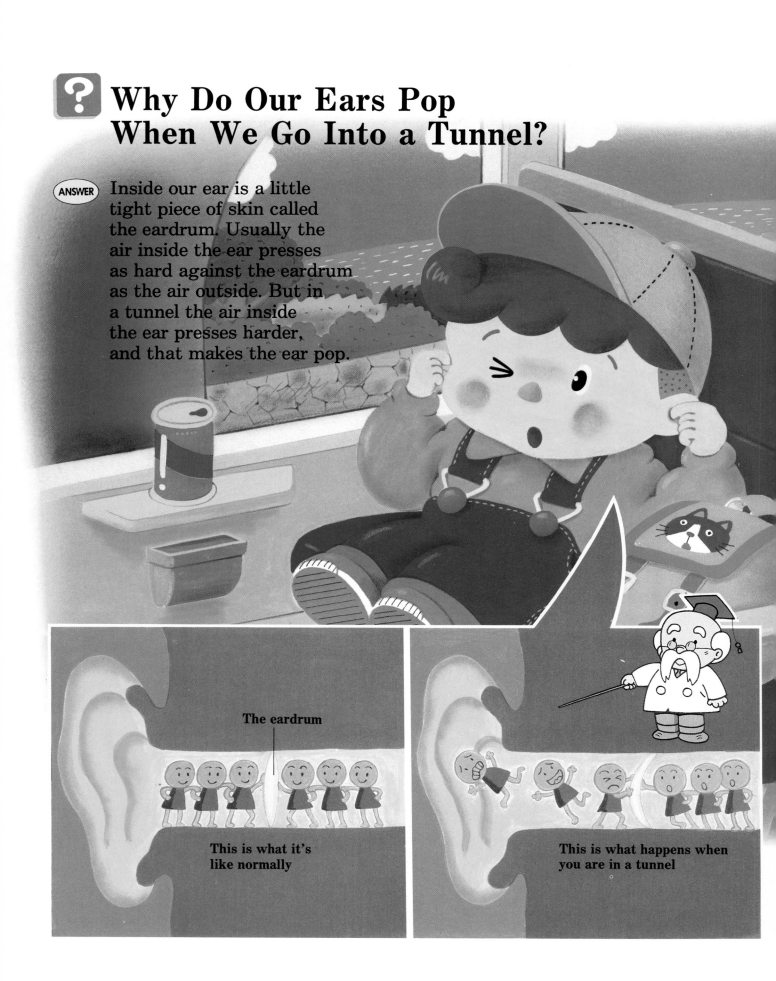

The eardrum

This is what it's like normally

This is what happens when you are in a tunnel

Why Do Our Ears Clog When We Blow Our Nose?

Our ear and nose are joined by a tube. When we blow our nose, air is forced into the tube. Air pressure on our eardrum is then out of balance, and our ear feels clogged.

■ How to fix clogged ears

When the air pressure on both sides of our eardrum balances, the eardrum pops into place. To make this happen faster, try swallowing or yawning.

Fix aluminum foil tightly on one end of a tube. Put your mouth at the other end and breathe in and out. The foil will move the way your eardrum does when the air pressure on your ear changes.

● **To the Parent**

The eardrum is a very thin membrane, only .004 of an inch (0.1 mm) thick. In normal circumstances the air pressure on it from the middle ear is about the same as pressure from the outside. When the outside air pressure is suddenly reduced—as when entering a tunnel—the narrowness of the ear passage does not allow the air pressure in the inner ear to adjust at once, and our ears are uncomfortable until it does.

❓ Why Does Our Nose Run?

ANSWER Inside our nose is a moist lining. It is called the mucous membrane. When we catch a cold the lining dries out. Our body produces water to make the lining healthy, and that makes our nose run. Our nose also runs when we cry. The nose and eyes are connected by a tube. When we cry it overflows and tears run down our nose.

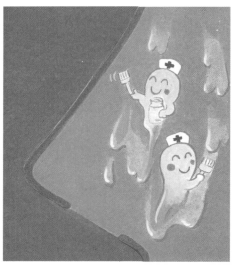

The water that comes from our nose when we have a cold is nature's way of helping heal the tissues deep in our nose. It makes them strong and well.

AH-CHoo!

A narrow tube connects our eyes and our nose.

When we cry and shed tears, our nose usually runs a little bit at the same time.

● **To the Parent**

When we catch a cold, the mucous membrane in the nose becomes irritated by the virus. The tissues of the membrane try to kill the virus by increasing their production of water from the blood and the leukocytes, or white corpuscles, that will actually attack the virus. That is the reason our nose runs when we catch cold. Also, mucus that the mucous membrane secretes is continuously being moved toward our nostrils by the action of numerous extremely minute hairs called cilia.

So Why Does Dirt Come Out of Our Nose?

There is a sticky mucous membrance in the nose. It oozes mucus, which runs down toward the tip of the nose. All the germs and dust that fly in the air are caught by this mucus. The sticky mucus and the dirt it has caught come out when we blow our nose.

What Happens When We Lose a Tooth?

ANSWER Children's first teeth sit on top of their grown-up teeth. In a few years the big teeth push the baby teeth out. This happens only one time. When our big teeth push through we must take good care of them because we get only one set of big teeth.

■ How teeth grow

The grown-up tooth on the bottom starts small, but it soon pushes the baby tooth out.

Let's Count Our Teeth

Grown-ups have more teeth than children do.

Children's teeth

Children have 20 teeth in all. The molars at the back don't grow out until much later.

Grown-ups' teeth

Grown-ups have 32 teeth in all.

■ Animals change teeth too

Animals such as horses and lions get new teeth one time in their lives, just like people, with the grown-up, or permanent, teeth growing up to push the baby teeth out. Snakes and crocodiles may get several sets of teeth during their lives.

Horses

Lions

Snakes

Crocodiles

● To the Parent

Children get their first milk teeth at about seven months and should have 20 of them when they are about three years old. At about age six they begin to get their adult teeth in the same order as their milk teeth. The molars also start to appear then. There are three on each side on both the top and bottom.

Why Do We Get Cavities?

ANSWER When food we eat sticks to our teeth it makes a place for germs to work. The food turns bad, and the germs multiply and make holes in our teeth, which we call cavities.

■ How we get cavities

Yummy-yummy! I'm going to eat lots!

Only a little more to go!

Oh, goody! Yummy-yummy!

Germs

We've made a big hole!

Let's make a big hole right here!

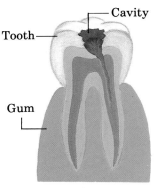

Cavity

Tooth

Gum

▲ Don't get this

We should always brush our teeth right after eating. But if we should happen to get a cavity anyway, then we should go to the dentist right away. If we don't, our teeth will become worse and worse and may have to be pulled if they're too bad.

■ These foods make cavities

Cake

Chocolate

Candy

Ice Cream

■ These foods make our teeth strong

Eggs

Fish

Shrimp

MILK

Milk

CHEESE

Cheese

● **To the Parent**

The surface of our teeth is made of enamel and is the hardest substance in our body. Beneath it is a layer of dentin. Inside that is the dental pulp, which contains blood vessels and nerves. When teeth start to decay and the material they are made of wears away, it affects that dental pulp and results in toothache. Cavities are caused when particles of food left in the mouth after eating begin to decay. This produces acid which eats away the enamel of teeth.

Do Animals Get Cavities Too?

Animals living in the wild don't get cavities. But animals that are kept by people and are given the same food that human beings eat might get cavities just as we do.

▼ **American badger.** Don't those look like cavities?

TRY THIS

When we clean our teeth, let's always make sure we clean the front and the back, the top and the bottom. It is very easy for food to get stuck at the top and bottom of our very back teeth, and even behind those back teeth. So you must pay attention to those back teeth. If you do this, your dentist will find fewer cavities.

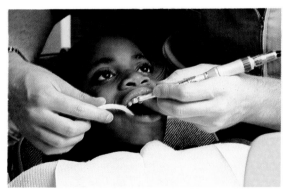

Blair Seitz/Photo Researchers, Inc.

Where Does Our Voice Come From?

 Our voice comes from deep in our throat. At the back of our throat is a tube called the larynx, and in this are two membranes called our vocal cords. Air passing in and out makes the vocal cords vibrate, and that is what gives us our voice. Our vocal cords are also what help our voice make melodies when we sing.

There are our vocal cords.

■ How voices are created

Our vocal cords are very thin membranes. When we speak, they move and change shape, and the space between them changes, too.

When we breathe, it opens wide.

When we talk, it gets smaller.

The same sort of membrane is fitted to a harmonica!

Boys' voices change when they become men

When boys are about thirteen years old their voices change and become deeper.

Harmonica

People have different voices. Here is where you'll find mine on a harmonica scale.

■ Different throats

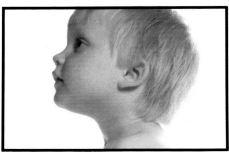

▲ A boy's

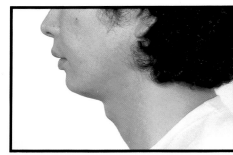

▲ **A man's.** As a male turns adult, part of the larynx, which contains the vocal cords, enlarges, and you can see it here. It is a man's Adam's apple.

● To the Parent

The vocal cords are a pair of elastic folds that lie in the mucous membrane that lines the larynx. During mere breathing they rest along the larynx walls, leaving the air passage open. When you speak they are stretched across the larynx, causing them to vibrate and produce voice. Various muscles adjust the tension on the cords to give the voice a higher or lower pitch. The tauter the cord, the higher the pitch.

? What Is a Uvula?

ANSWER Look in a mirror and open your mouth wide. Do you see a lump of fleshy tissue hanging from the top of your throat? That is your uvula. It is hanging from your soft palate.

■ How our throat works

In our throat is a tube called the windpipe, or trachea. It lets air get in and out of our lungs. Another tube, called the esophagus, brings food to our stomach. Your body must make sure that air and food go down the right tubes. Your soft palate and epiglottis help. You can see how this works in the pictures below.

When we breathe, tubes are open.

- Soft palate
- Uvula
- Esophagus
- Windpipe

Your throat directs food one way and air the other way.

When we swallow, they close.

- Uvula
  Blocks off the nose.
- Windpipe
  Epiglottis blocks it.
- Food
- Esophagus

■ If not for your soft palate...

COUGH!
COUGH!

Food or drink might go up the pathway that leads from your throat to your nose.

■ Without an epiglottis...

Food that goes down your throat might get stuck in your windpipe. This could prevent you from breathing.

● **To the Parent**

The uvula, in the back of your mouth, is attached to the end of the soft palate. As you swallow, the palate slides back and shuts off the passageway leading to your nose. At the same time your epiglottis closes off the path to your windpipe, or trachea. This keeps food out of your air passages and guides it toward the esophagus, which leads to your stomach.

■ Do animals have uvulas?

▲ **Gorilla.** Yes. You can see it.   ▲ **Hippo.** Look real hard; it's there!   ▲ **Angler fish.** No uvula for it.

39

❓ Why Do We Cough and Sneeze When We Catch Cold?

ANSWER When we catch cold a lot of germs collect in our nose and throat, and they make us feel bad. Our nose runs, and some yellow stuff called phlegm clogs up our throat. We cough and sneeze to try to clear our nose and our throat so we'll feel better.

We sneeze to clear our nose of germs. This blows out the germs and the runny stuff in our nose.

When we cough it helps clear out our throat. We also cough up gobs of phlegm.

Sometimes We Cough and Sneeze Even When We're Well

Sometimes, even if we don't have a cold, we might sneeze. We do it if we look into the sun, or smell pepper. We cough if food sticks in our throat when we are gobbling our food instead of eating right.

Sometimes it hurts when we cough

Coughing gets rid of germs so that we will feel better. But when you cough too much, your throat becomes irritated. Then it's a good idea to try not to cough quite so much.

When we feel that we are about to cough we should take in a slow, deep breath.

Or drink some warm water.

MINI-DATA

Block that germ

In some places people wear a mask when they have a cold to keep their germs from flying out and giving colds to other people.

● To the Parent

The nasal cavities, the pharynx, trachea and other organs through which air passes constitute what is known as the respiratory tract. When we catch cold, the mucous membrane in these passages gets inflamed and secretes a great deal of mucus. This causes the system to become clogged with phlegm and nasal fluid, and this in turn further irritates the nerves of the respiratory tract, causing us to cough and sneeze.

❓ How Many Bones Are There in Our Body?

ANSWER We have 206 bones in our body. These bones fit together to make our skeleton. The largest bone is in our legs. The smallest ones are in our ears. As shown by the X-ray photos on the page at right, various animals have skeletons that are much the same as people have.

MINI-DATA

Babies are bonier

Newborn babies have more than 300 bones. As the child grows, some of these grow together to make bigger bones, and the number of bones decreases.

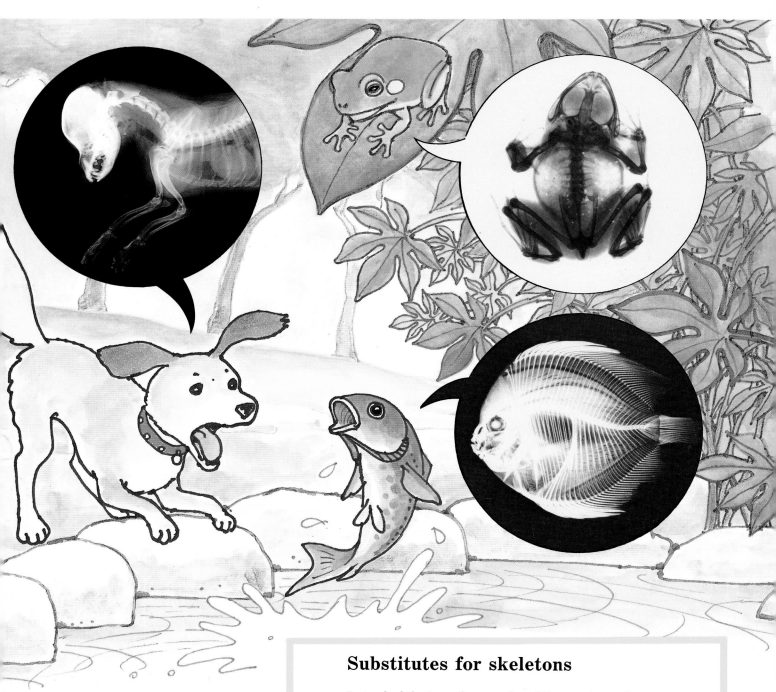

Substitutes for skeletons

Instead of the bony frameworks of the creatures shown above, some animals have shells of one kind or another, which serve both to protect them and to hold their bodies together. Among them are insects, crustaceans and shellfish.

A beetle

A lobster

● **To the Parent**

The human form gets its shape from a skeleton consisting of 206 bones held together by flexible tissue made up of cartilage and ligaments. This framework of living material accommodates large size and also provides for freedom of movement. It is typical of all the vertebrate animals. In addition to extending support, the skeleton allows for the attachment of the muscles used in movement and furnishes protection for vital organs like the brain and lungs.

❓ Why Do We Get Hungry?

ANSWER We get hungry when our stomach becomes empty. Just after we eat, our stomach is full, but our body digests the food and our stomach becomes empty again. When all the food is out of the stomach we get hungry.

Our stomach feels full for about an hour after we have eaten.

After about three hours, there is less food in our stomach.

Then Why Does Our Stomach Rumble?

Our stomach and our intestines, which you see in the drawing below, are moving all the time because they are digesting our food. When all the food is gone there is nothing but air. This air gets pushed around by the tummy and intestines, and that is what makes all those noises.

● **To the Parent**

We usually feel hungry if there is no food in the stomach, but we might also feel hunger pangs if our blood sugar becomes low. Hunger is registered by the hypothalamus in the brain. This important supervisory center regulates many body functions and is sensitive to increases and decreases in our blood sugar level. This relates to the amount of nutrition contained in the blood at a given time.

After about five hours, most of the food has been used up.

After about six hours, there is almost nothing in our stomach.

Why Do Foods Taste Different?

(ANSWER) Our tongue is covered with thousands of tiny taste buds. They can recognize four tastes: sweet, salty, sour and bitter. When food mixes in our mouth, these different buds send messages to the brain, which tells us how things taste.

Yum! This tastes sweet!

Yuck!! Lemons taste sour!

■ Let's find out about taste

▶ Wipe your tongue with a towel so that it is dry. Now put a little sugar on the dry part. You will not be able to taste it. Your tongue must be wet for your taste buds to work.

In its normal position inside the mouth our tongue is moist so it can taste things.

▲ Put some salt water on the back of your tongue. You can hardly taste it. Now put it on the front. It tastes very salty. Different taste buds are located on different parts of your tongue. So tastes are stronger in some spots than in others.

▲ Your sense of smell helps you taste things. Hold your nose tight so that you can't smell anything. Now put a piece of onion on your tongue. You can barely taste it. But as soon as you let go of your nose you'll find that the taste seems much stronger.

47

Why Does Our Stomach Ache If We Play Right After Eating?

ANSWER When we eat some food, our stomach starts to digest it. To do this the stomach needs oxygen, so blood rushes to the stomach to give it the oxygen. If we start to play just then, other parts of our body will need more oxygen. When the blood carries oxygen away from the stomach for the other body parts, we get a stomachache.

If we play games just after we eat, the blood our stomach needs to digest the food we have eaten is used by other body organs.

When we eat, a lot of blood goes to our stomach to help it digest the food.

Take it easy

The best thing to do is to rest for a little while after eating and not jump about.

Even if our blood has gone to other places in our body, our stomach is working hard, and that's what gives us a stomachache!

❓ Why Do We Gain Weight?

 ANSWER We eat food to give us energy and make our bodies strong. If we eat more than our body needs and don't exercise enough, the food we eat will not be used up as energy. Instead, it will be stored in our body as fat, and we will gain weight.

■ This can make you fat

Just look at this boy eat! He's really gobbling his food. Then he doesn't get any exercise. Instead, he lies in front of the television set and dreams about eating more food. That's why he weighs more than he should.

Walking and other types of exercise help people lose weight.

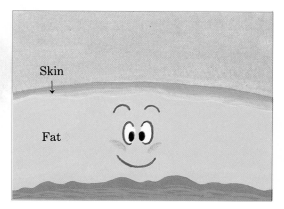

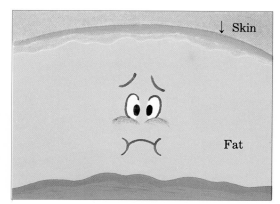

People who are too heavy have much more fat under their skin than people who are not.

High in calories

Rice

Bread

Sweets

Fat meat

Butter

Low in calories

Vegetables

Nonfat yogurt

Bean curd

Fish

In order to be healthy, it is important to eat a wide variety of good foods. Some foods have more calories than other foods. High-calorie foods give your body lots of energy. But if you eat more of these foods than your body needs then you will gain weight.

● **To the Parent**

Although obesity can be attributed to a number of factors, it is generally accepted that the main cause is overeating—that is, too great an intake of calories. If the energy provided by our food intake exceeds the amount spent in exercise, we will get fat. In a minority of cases, however, obesity stems from such causes as heredity or an imbalance in hormone secretion.

Why Do We Make Fingerprints?

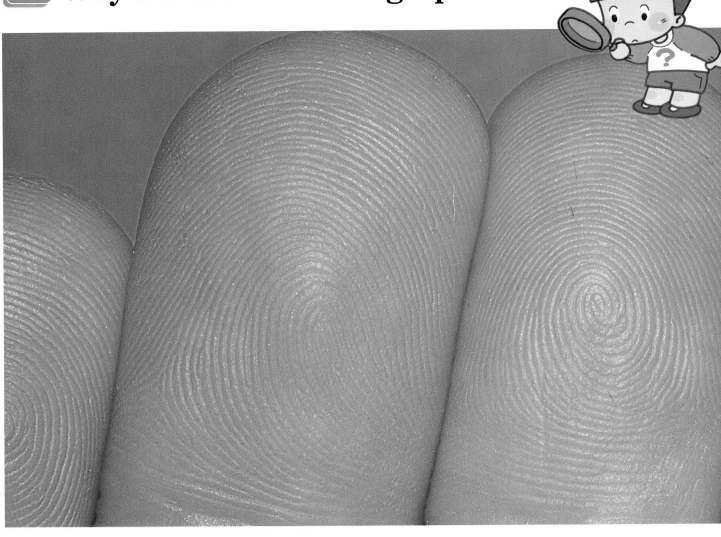

ANSWER The lines on our fingers that make fingerprints also help us grip things and hold them firmly so that we don't drop them. No two people's prints are the same. That means that nobody else has the same fingerprints as you have. And your print of today will be the same when you get very old.

■ Chimpanzees have fingerprints, too!

Now you know that people have fingerprints, but did you know that some animals also have them? Chimpanzees have hands that are sort of like ours, and they have fingerprints that are like ours, too. The way that their hands are made gives them the prints, but it also helps them pick fruit and hang onto the branches of trees. Their fingerprints go farther down their fingers than people's do, too. Right down to the end of their fingers. Some other animals that live in trees, such as squirrels, have fingerprints just the same as people do.

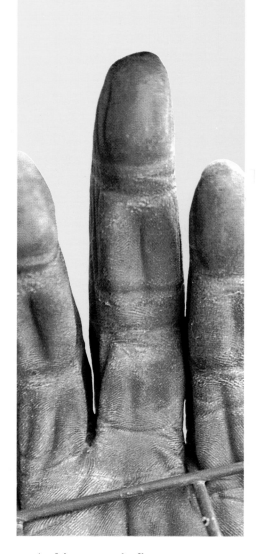

▲ **A chimpanzee's fingers**

Can you see how their fingerprints are like ours? Can you see how they are different?

● **To the Parent**

So far as is known, no two people have fingerprints that are the same, and for that reason prints are used to identify people. Prints may be looped, whorled or arched, based on the configuration of the ridges at the tips of the fingers. Patterns of fingerprints never change.

MINI-DATA

We have prints not only on our fingers but on our toes as well. The lines and grooves on the bottom of our toes and feet are meant to keep us from slipping. They are part of the things that nature gave people before they first wore shoes.

Footprints too

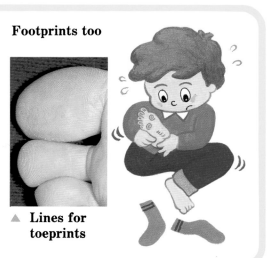

▲ **Lines for toeprints**

Why Do Our Nails Grow?

ANSWER Nails are formed in a place called the nail root. They are being formed all the time. Slowly they are pushed out from the root and this is why they grow. We have nails to protect the tops of our fingers.

This is the bone in a finger.

A nail root is like a factory. This is where our nails form.

How Long Does It Take Our Nails to Grow?

Nails grow about .04 inch (1 mm) in about 10 days. Children's nails grow faster than grown-ups', and everyone's nails grow faster in hot weather than when it's cold.

Children's nails grow faster than grown-ups'.

Nails grow faster when the weather is hot.

It's best to keep nails cut short

If you don't keep your nails cut short, they will break, and they can scratch, too. Also it is bad to get dirt under your nails. That is unhealthy. So when your nails start to get long, cut them short. And always keep your nails clean.

MINI-DATA

At the base of your nails is a white crescent moon shape. This is where the nail grows from, and the white crescent is the new nail. Sometimes if you are not well, you may not be able to see this crescent-shaped nail.

Broken nails

Dirty nails

● To the Parent

Nails are formed from skin that has hardened. The part of the nail buried under the skin where the nail is formed is called the root, and the part that grows out is called the body of the nail. The nail is still soft when it is formed at the root but hardens as it emerges. Where the nail emerges is a white crescent. This shows where the nail is still semi-hard.

? Why Does Our Skin Wrinkle When We Take a Bath?

▲ A wrinkled hand

ANSWER The skin on the inside of our hands and the bottom of our feet is thicker than the skin on other parts of our body. When it has been in water a long time it gets spongy. The fingernail at the tip of your finger stops it from swelling that way, so the finger wrinkles.

Cell

Our whole body is made of millions and millions of tiny things called cells. When we take a bath, the cells in the skin of our fingers and toes soak up water and swell up. There isn't room for these swollen cells to lie side by side like they usually do. They have to bunch up like those below, and that's what causes our skin to wrinkle.

The cells become swollen up and bunched together, and that is what causes wrinkles.

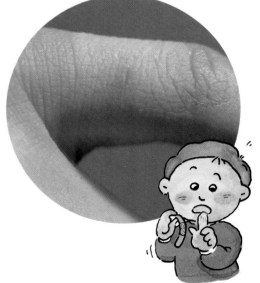

▲ A wrinkled foot

■ What a bandage does

If you take a tape bandage off an injury the skin underneath will be white. That is because water that was trapped in the skin by the bandage has caused the skin to swell and turn white just as it does when you have been in the bath a long time.

● **To the Parent**

Compared with other parts of the body, the skin on the palm of the hand and the bottom of the feet is particularly thick. When it becomes swollen and spongy from being in water a long time, the surface area of this skin expands significantly. The dermis (the skin below), however, remains unchanged, and so the epidermis (the skin surface), is forced to wrinkle.

Why Do We Sweat When We Get Hot?

(ANSWER) We sweat when we get hot because sweating helps cool down our body. If we didn't sweat, our body would get hotter and hotter. We would get dizzy and faint, and could become very ill.

I'm a drop of sweat. It's my job to carry the heat out of your body!

Heat

Sweat

58

We sweat all the time

We don't sweat just when we get hot. We always sweat. We sweat when we are asleep and even when we are just standing still. We sweat all the time.

Heat leaves our body all the time, even when we're sweating a little bit.

How much do we sweat?

We sweat more when it's hot than when it's cold, and more at play than when we're idle. But most of us sweat enough in a day to fill four or five small milk bottles.

And Why Is Sweat So Salty?

You already know that your body contains a lot of water, but did you know that it also contains a lot of salt? Sweat is a mixture of water and salt, and that is why it tastes salty. If you sweat a lot, when the water in the sweat dries out it will leave traces of salt on your clothing and even on your skin.

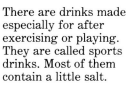

Salt

Your body needs salt. But when you play, it loses a lot of its salt.

There are drinks made especially for after exercising or playing. They are called sports drinks. Most of them contain a little salt.

• To the Parent

Sweating reduces our body temperature because heat leaves the body with the sweat. This is nature's way of regulating our body temperature. If the day is warm, or if you exercise, you generally begin to sweat to lower your body temperature. When sweat on the outside of your body dries, the process of the evaporation also cools your body. If a person did not sweat, the body would keep heating up and heatstroke might result.

❓ Why Do We Shiver When We Are Cold?

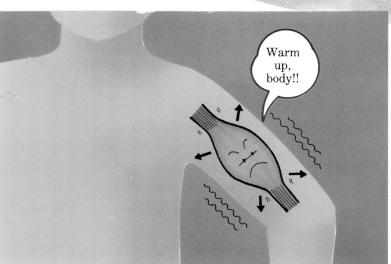

Warm up, body!!

ANSWER We feel cold because the heat in our body has gone down. This is called our temperature. Our muscles shiver and shake to make our body warm up again. But you can also make yourself warm by moving around and exercising your body.

■ Body temperatures

People, animals and birds always have the same body temperature even if the air temperature is different. Snakes and lizards lose heat when the air is cold. They will sleep until it gets warm.

98.6°F. (37°C.)

97.7°F. (36.5°C.)

100°F. (37.8°C.)

106.7°F. (41.5°C.)

The temperature of snakes and lizards changes with the air that surrounds them.

Why Do We Get Goose Bumps?

A long time ago when people had hair on their bodies, they would fluff it up to keep warm when it was cold. People today do not have so much hair, but the pores where hair would come out stand up and make goose bumps instead.

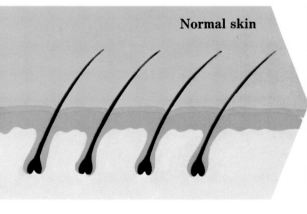

Normal skin

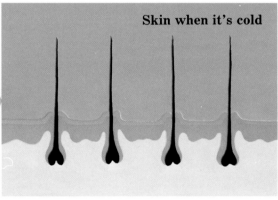

Skin when it's cold

When it's cold our hair stands up straight like the hairs in the blue. The skin around each hair swells up and closes the pore tightly so the heat of our body cannot escape.

● To the Parent

The human body is continuously kept in a stable condition mainly through the function of the autonomic nervous system and the body's hormones. The medical term for this is maintaining homeostasis. Whatever the climatic conditions, this keeps the body at a constant temperature of about 98.6°F. (37°C.). In cold weather the body needs a bit more body heat, and it generates as much as is necessary by causing the muscles to contract into the spasms that we commonly refer to as shivers.

61

Why Do We Get Sunburned or Tanned?

ANSWER Our skin contains lots of little black grains called melanin. They protect us from rays of the sun that might harm us. When the sun is very hot they increase in number to block out the harmful rays. They are near the surface of the skin, so when the number of them increases, the skin gets dark. We call that a tan. If there is not enough melanin, the skin will get sunburned and turn red.

▲ **Tanned children.** Ultraviolet rays are very strong near the ocean, so we brown quickly when we play there.

• To the Parent

The skin has an outer layer called the epidermis and an inner layer, the dermis (derm), also called the true skin, with a layer of tissue below both. The cells that produce melanin are between the dermis and epidermis. Melanin protects the body from the sun's harmful ultraviolet rays. Thus the stronger the sunlight hitting us, the more melanin the body produces to screen out the ultraviolet.

Ultraviolet rays are bad for us. If our body is exposed to them too long it will become burned.

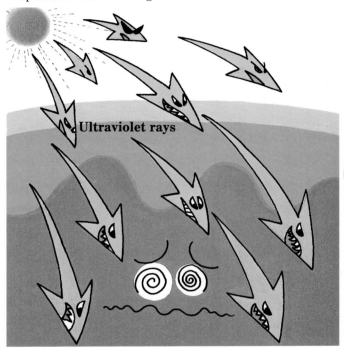

Ultraviolet rays

■ Sunburn really hurts

If we stay too long in the sun when our skin is still white, we will turn red and our skin will hurt. That's because the sun is hot enough to burn us. It also means we don't have enough melanin in our body to protect us. People who don't have much melanin in their body burn easily.

62

When our body is exposed to ultraviolet light it makes more melanin to guard our skin from the rays.

Melanin

When our body produces lots of melanin our skin will turn brown. It protects us from the harmful rays.

And Why Does Our Skin Peel if We Get Too Much Sun?

When we are out in the sun the melanin in our body will increase to protect us, but too much sun will damage the topmost layer of skin. After a while that outside layer of skin will peel off.

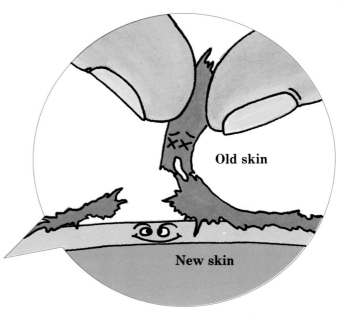

Old skin

New skin

The old skin won't peel and flake away until the new skin underneath is all ready to take its place.

? Why Do We Have Moles?

We are little bits of melanin that have come together

ANSWER Sometimes a lot of the melanin that we have in our body comes together and stays in one place a little under the surface of our skin. That's what we call a mole. Moles can be any size. There are small ones and large ones. Some might even stick out the way a wart does. But up to now nobody has learned exactly why we have them.

They say that if a mother and father have a lot of moles, their children will probably have them too.

Moles do not disappear as we grow older.

64

And Why Do We Get Freckles?

We freckle from staying in the sun a long time.

Like moles, freckles occur when a lot of melanin is concentrated in one spot.

Light-complexioned people freckle fast. Dark skins do not freckle so easily.

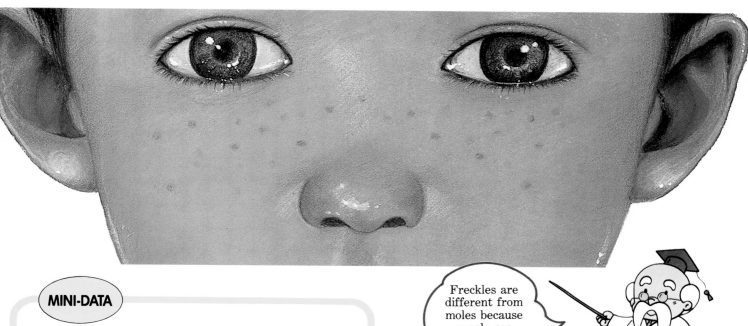

MINI-DATA

As many people grow older, they get brown blotches on their faces and their hands. These are also caused by lots of melanin coming together in one place. Some people call these blotches aging spots.

Freckles are different from moles because people can lose freckles as they grow.

• **To the Parent**

Moles form where there has been discoloration of the skin. Few babies have them at birth, but they begin to appear in children about three or four years old. Moles may be caused by disorder in pigmentation cells or blood vessels. They come in many different sizes and may be flat or raised.

Why Do We Pant When We Run?

 ANSWER We are breathing all the time. When we breathe, we take air into our lungs, which take out the oxygen and supply it to the rest of our body.

When we run we need more oxygen than at other times. That's why we breathe in shorter, faster gasps. This is what we call panting.

We take shorter, quicker breaths when we run.

We breathe much more slowly when we are walking.

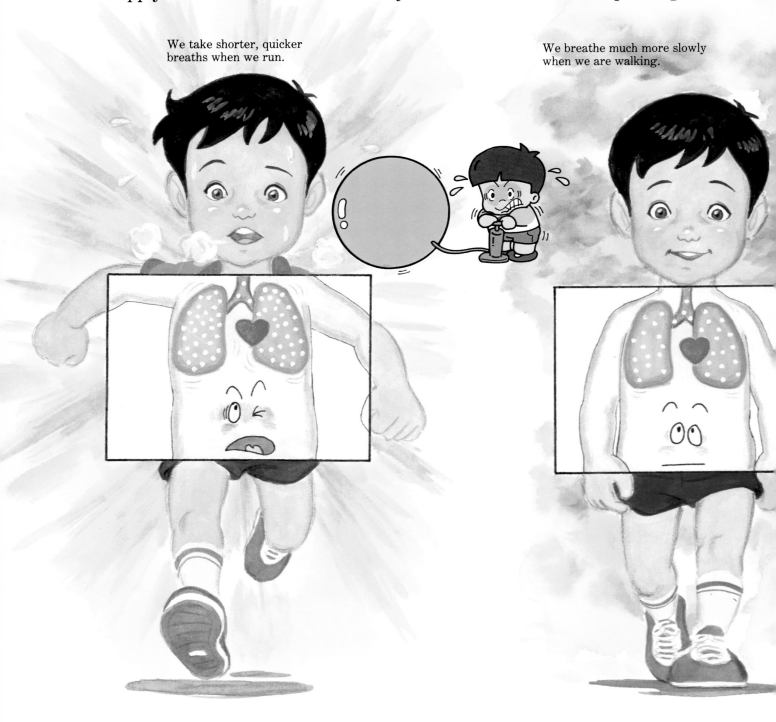

We breathe slowly when we walk because we don't need as much oxygen as when we are running. We need even less when we are asleep, so we breathe even more slowly then!

● **To the Parent**

Respiration is the name for the process through which oxygen is drawn into, and carbon dioxide is expelled from, the body. It is controlled by the respiratory center, which is located in the medulla oblongata. This center responds to an increase of carbon dioxide and depletion of oxygen in the blood, brought on by strenuous exercise, by causing respiration to accelerate.

When we are sleeping we breathe easily and quietly.

? Why Do We Get Hiccups?

ANSWER Between your stomach and chest is a sheet of muscle called the diaphragm. Usually the diaphragm moves up and down at a steady pace to make you breathe. But sometimes the diaphragm twitches, causing a sudden intake of air that results in the familiar hiccup sound. No one knows for sure why we get hiccups, but they sometimes happen when we eat or drink too much or too fast.

This passage past our vocal cords is closed, but air still gets by, and that is what makes us hiccup.

Our diaphragm lies here, just below our lungs and above our stomach. Here it is twitching.

The Diaphragm at Work

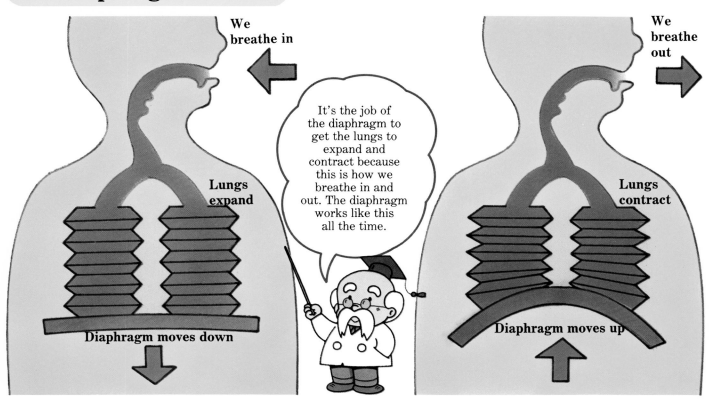

We breathe in

Lungs expand

Diaphragm moves down

It's the job of the diaphragm to get the lungs to expand and contract because this is how we breathe in and out. The diaphragm works like this all the time.

We breathe out

Lungs contract

Diaphragm moves up

■ Here are some ways to stop hiccups

We don't know a definite way to stop hiccups, but here are some things you can try that sometimes work.

Hold your nose and drink a glass of water.

Hold your breath for as long as you can.

● To the Parent

A hiccup occurs when a spasmodic contraction of the diaphragm causes an unexpected intake of air. This causes the epiglottis to snap shut suddenly, which makes the characteristic "hic" sound that gives the phenomenon its name. It frequently occurs when we eat something hot or cold. There is no foolproof method of stopping hiccups, although there are any number of supposed cures. In most cases hiccups will stop naturally after a time.

Why Do Our Legs Go to Sleep If We Sit on Them?

ANSWER When we sit like this for a long time, the weight of our upper body presses against our blood vessels and nerves. When our nerves are squeezed like this, they let our body know it by going to sleep.

Blood vessels

Nerves

Sitting like this squashes your nerves and blood vessels.

Your nerves let you know that they are numb by their tingling.

■ If we sit too long...

If we sit with our body weight on our legs for a long time, we squash our nerves so badly that they go to sleep completely. The feeling in our legs disappears except for a sharp tingling sensation.

■ How to get numb

■ How not to

● **To the Parent**

The major cause of numbness is severe pressure on the leg nerves. In this position, the instep is pressed flat against the floor and, since there is hardly any flesh on the instep, the nerves tend to be severely compressed between the hard surface and the bones of the instep. Pressure on nerves spreads until the entire leg finally goes numb.

Why Are We Ticklish?

ANSWER We laugh when someone touches us lightly with a feather or pokes us in a spot where we are ticklish. Below our skin are special nerve endings. When we are tickled, the nerves send a message to the brain. Because we are ticklish, we know when things are touching our skin.

Some people are more ticklish than others, but we are not sure why.

■ We feel other things too

Some nerves feel the heat of a warm bath. Others feel the winter's cold.

TRY THIS

There are ways that you can fool your sense of touch. Here is one of them: Put some water and some ice cubes in one container, and stir until the water gets very cold. Put some cool water in a second container. Put your hand into the ice water and leave it there for about a minute. Then take it out and quickly put it into the cool water in the other container. You may be surprised: The cool water will feel very warm.

Some nerves are there so that we can feel pain. This is a warning signal that our body is hurt.

● **To the Parent**

Humans respond to a variety of sensations through an intricate network of nerves. Sensations are measured below the skin by special organs called receptors. These are minute structures at the end of hairlike nerve fibers. These endings are specialized to feel the sensations of touch, pressure, temperature and pain. Receptors are grouped according to function. Fingertips have many receptors for touch but few for heat or cold. Thus we test a baby's bath by running water on the wrist rather than on the fingers. The sense of touch provides a warning when there is a threat to the body. Pain is a signal that immediate steps are necessary to avoid damage to body tissue. Often, though, pain elicits a reflex response from the body even before the brain becomes aware of pain.

❓ Why Do We Yawn?

ANSWER When we are tired or bored, and our brain is a bit dull because it is not getting enough oxygen, we yawn. Our mouth opens and we gulp in a lot of air. That way we send some extra oxygen to the brain and feel better.

■ A yawn is a deep breath we take unintentionally

▼ When we are tired or bored...

• **To the Parent**

If we are tired and the flow of blood to the brain becomes sluggish we don't get enough oxygen, and the amount of carbon dioxide in the blood increases. As a result we feel sleepy. At such times as this the respiratory center in the brain makes us yawn. That in turn makes us open our mouth wide and also sends a stimulus from the masticatory muscles to the brain. Thus we get additional oxygen, and that makes our brain clear up and we become awake again.

In the corner of our eye is a little tube that leads to our nose. At the top of it is a small container that is called a lachrymal sac. It holds our tears. Lachrymal always means something to do with tears. At times when we yawn, the muscles in our face squeeze this sac and tears come out, so we get tears in our eyes.

Here's a picture of your lachrymal sac, or tear holder. As you can see, it is between your eye and your nose. See the tear spill out.

Lachrymal sac

▼ That's when we yawn.

■ **Animals also yawn!**

▶ **Cats do**

▶ **Dogs too**

Why Do We Get Sleepy at Night?

Day

Night

ANSWER During the day we are doing all sorts of things, and so our brain works very hard. At night things slow down and get quiet. After its busy day our brain is tired, so we get sleepy.

But Some Nights We Just Don't Feel Sleepy

Grown-ups who get up and go to work at night don't feel sleepy then. They sleep during the day.

When we are excited and looking forward to something we're going to do the next day, we may find it rather hard to get to sleep at night.

■ As we get older we need less sleep per day

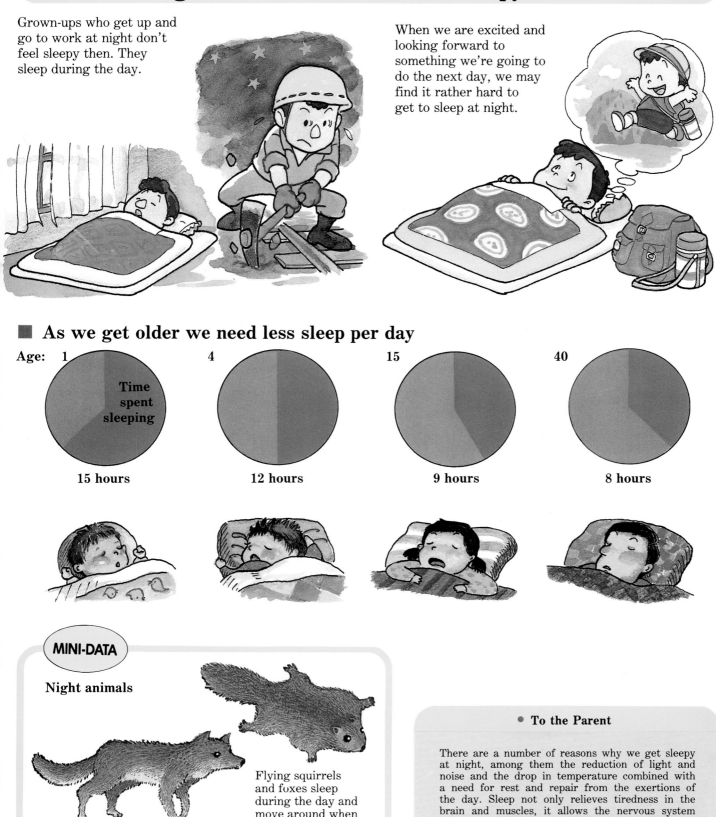

Age: 1

Time spent sleeping

15 hours

4

12 hours

15

9 hours

40

8 hours

MINI-DATA

Night animals

Flying squirrels and foxes sleep during the day and move around when it becomes dark.

● **To the Parent**

There are a number of reasons why we get sleepy at night, among them the reduction of light and noise and the drop in temperature combined with a need for rest and repair from the exertions of the day. Sleep not only relieves tiredness in the brain and muscles, it allows the nervous system and the organs it controls to restore some of the energy they have expended during the day.

Why Do We Have Dreams?

ANSWER Sometimes though we're sound asleep our brain may still be a little bit awake. They say that is when we have dreams. We have dreams about things that happened to us during the day, or things we always think about, but nobody really knows why we dream.

MINI-DATA

We believe that animals like dogs have dreams, too.

And Why Do We Talk in Our Sleep?

When we talk in our sleep we usually do it when we are having a dream. If we are talking in the dream, and we say it out loud, that's talking in our sleep.

OoH HELP!

The things we dream about are sometimes things that we have done during the day or things that we think about quite a bit.

If we talk in our sleep it is perhaps because we are having a bad dream.

● To the Parent

It is said that things in our subconscious may appear in our dreams, or that dreams may be caused by external stimuli such as light and sound, and pressure directly affecting the brain while we are asleep. Studies of our brain waves during sleep indicate that every one and a half to two hours our sleep gets shallower and that this is the time when we seem to dream most.

? What Is It?

■ Hair

Hair grows out through our skin. The roots of our hair are under the skin and are the places where oil is made and hair is produced.

■ A tongue

The surface of our tongue is made up of lots of little points. Just below the tips of these points is where our sense of taste is.

■ Eyelashes

Eyelashes help to stop dust and dirt from getting in our eyes. Eyelashes are very sensitive, and if even the tiniest bit of dust touches them they will flutter and brush it away. The top lashes, as you know, are much longer than the bottom ones.

Growing-Up Album

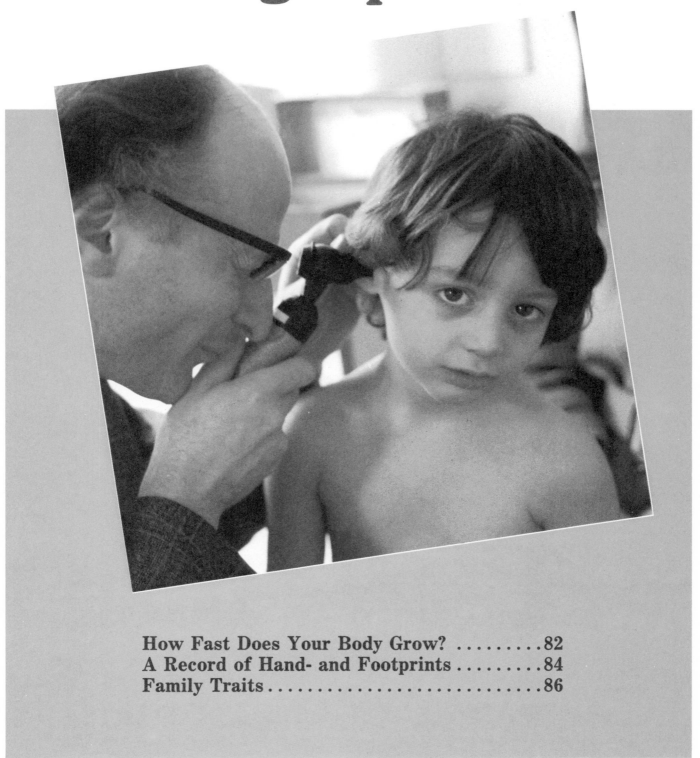

How Fast Does Your Body Grow?

Use the charts below to record the development of your children.

Children grow up so fast. Before you realize it they have acquired numerous locomotive skills. We usually record some sudden dramatic progress like the day baby took his or her first step. But wouldn't it be a good idea to record other important events like when a child first climbed the stairs or the day he or she was able to stand on one leg? Keeping track on a graph of how tall your children have grown and how much they weigh might make an interesting and worthwhile record.

■ Early milestones of locomotive skills

Baby first crawled

Took first step

Learned to climb stairs

■ Watch them grow

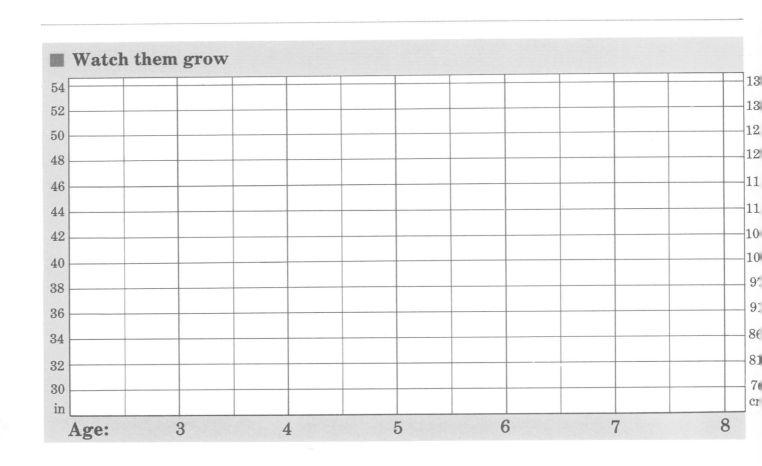

■ Other locomotive skills

When your child gets past three years old, he or she will be able to do quite a number of things. Walk on tiptoes, for instance. Or walk in a narrow space without stepping to one side or another. Walking backward. Being able to swing on a swing without help. Being able to catch a large ball. Or, finally, learning how to skip.

Balanced on one leg without help

Rode a tricycle

■ Got milk teeth; lost them

It's a good idea to make a note of when your child first got his or her milk teeth, and the order in which they grew. And it's also interesting to know when the teeth came out.

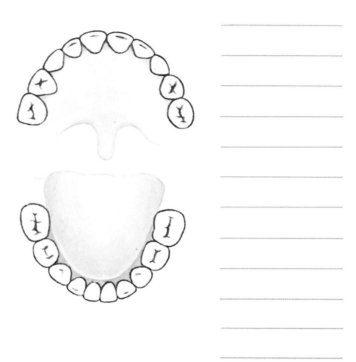

■ A handy weight chart

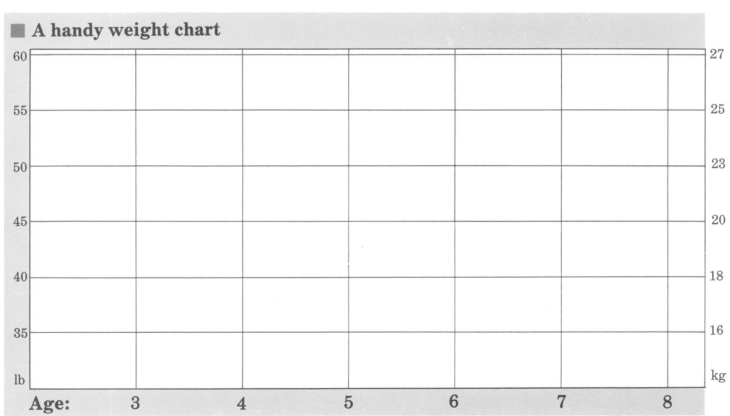

A Record of Hand- and Footprints

Children grow very quickly. Keeping a record of their height and weight is fine, but this is usually just a record of figures, or some marks made on a wall or chart. A record of handprints and footprints can be fun because you can actually see the shape of the hands or feet and how big they were the last time you measured them. And seeing them will make your children aware of how they have grown.

Making the prints

Making an outline by drawing around them is a good way.

You can dab the child's hand on a stamp pad that can be washed off and then apply the hand to paper or cloth.

Or using a washable ink and absorbent paper will do well.

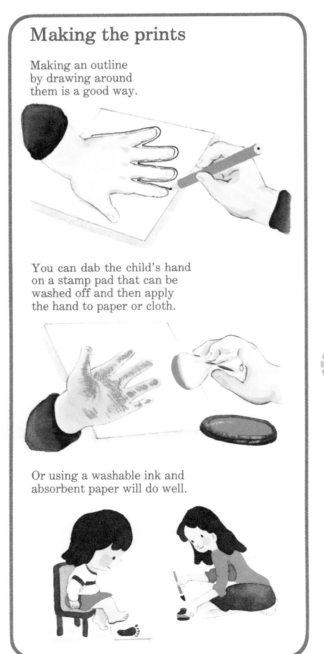

■ Children's questions

Children have a million and one questions about their own bodies. As children grow their questions will become different. You may find it interesting to keep a record of what they ask. This record will be more meaningful in later years if you record the age at which your child asked each question.

Family Traits

Many characteristics are passed down through families, while others are not. It is very interesting for a child to see how he or she is like other family members. Have your child paste pictures of family members in the boxes below. Then fill in the information. Have your child describe some of the ways family members are alike or different.

Paste photo here

Color of eyes

Color of hair

Curly or straight hair

Left- or right-handed

Name

Relationship to child

Other traits

Blood type

A Child's First Library of Learning

Our Bodies

Time-Life Books Inc. is a wholly owned subsidiary of Time Incorporated.
Time-Life Books, Alexandria, Virginia
Children's Publishing

Director:	Robert H. Smith
Associate Director:	R. S. Wotkyns III
Editorial Director:	Neil Kagan
Promotion Director:	Kathleen Tresnak
Editorial Consultants:	Jacqueline A. Ball
	Andrew Gutelle

Editorial Supervision by:
International Editorial Services Inc.
Tokyo, Japan

Editor:	C. E. Berry
Editorial Research:	Miki Ishii
Design:	Kim Bolitho
Writer:	Pauline Bush
Educational Consultants:	Janette Bryden
	Laurie Hanawa
Translation:	Ronald K. Jones

TIME LIFE ®

Library of Congress Cataloging-in-Publication Data

Our body.
   Our bodies.
      p.   cm.—(A Child's first library of learning)
   Originally published: Our body. 1989, c1988.
   Summary: Questions and answers present information about such aspects of our body as senses, emotions, growing, fitness, dental care, babies, and sexuality.
   ISBN 0-8094-9450-7.—ISBN 0-8094-9451-5.—ISBN 0-8094-9452-3.—ISBN 0-8094-9453-1
   1. Body, Human—Juvenile literature. [1. Body, Human—Miscellanea. 2. Questions and answers.] I. Time-Life Books. II. Title. III. Series.
[QP37.088 1991]
612—dc20   90-27404
©1988 Time-Life Books Inc.   CIP
©1983 Gakken Co. Ltd.   AC

Sixth printing 1993. Printed in U.S.A.
Published simultaneously in Canada.

TIME-LIFE is a trademark of Time Incorporated U.S.A.